Spiritual S.W.O.T. Analysis

A Companion to the Book for Self-Reflection, Leadership Development & Spiritual Growth

By Christopher D. Briwder, Sr.

CDBRIWDER
MINISTRIES

Spiritual S.W.O.T. Analysis - Workbook
A Companion to the Book for Self-reflection, Leadership Development & Spiritual Growth

Copyright © 2025 by **Christopher D. Briwder, Sr.**

All rights reserved. No part of this book may be reproduced, stored in a retrieval system, or transmitted in any form or by any means—electronic, mechanical, photocopying, recording, or otherwise—without prior written permission of the author, except for brief quotations used in reviews or articles.

Scripture quotations are taken from the **King James Version (KJV)** of the Bible.

Published by
C. D. Briwder Ministries

[Bartlett, Tennessee]

Section 1 — Foundations

1. Welcome & How to Use This Workbook

Welcome to the Spiritual S.W.O.T. Analysis Workbook. This tool is designed to help you reflect honestly, grow spiritually, and align your life with God's plan.

Use this workbook prayerfully, patiently, and consistently as you walk through each section.

2. What Is Spiritual S.W.O.T. Analysis?

S.W.O.T. stands for Strengths, Weaknesses, Opportunities, and Threats. This workbook uses the framework to strengthen spiritual awareness and growth.

3. Biblical Foundation for Self-Examination

Lamentations 3:40 — Let us search and try our ways, and turn again to the LORD.

Psalm 139:23–24 — Search me, O God, and know my heart…

2 Corinthians 13:5 — Examine yourselves, whether ye be in the faith…

4. Worksheet: Where Am I Spiritually?

Spiritual Area	1	2	3	4	5
Prayer Life					
Bible Reading					
Worship Life					
Faith/Trust					
Obedience					
Consistency					
Boundaries					
Emotional Health					
Accountability					
Serving Others					

Reflections:

_____

_____

_____

_____

5. Spiritual Habits Checklist

Prayer:

☐ I pray daily

☐ I pray when I wake up

☐ I pray before major decisions

☐ I pray through difficult emotions

☐ I pray for others regularly

Bible Reading:

☐ I read Scripture daily

☐ I study the Word

☐ I meditate on Scripture

☐ I apply what I read

Worship:

☐ I worship outside church

☐ I cultivate God's presence

☐ Worship resets me emotionally

Spiritual Community:

☐ I attend church consistently

☐ I am connected to ministry

☐ I have accountability

Lifestyle:

☐ I avoid things that pull me from God

☐ I guard my media intake

☐ I forgive quickly

☐ I walk in integrity

Reflections:

_____
_____
_____
_____
_____
_____
_____
_____

Section 2 — Session 1: Self-Assessment & Spiritual Awareness

1. Teaching Content: Understanding Spiritual Awareness

Spiritual awareness is the ability to recognize God's presence, your own spiritual condition, and the influences shaping your growth. Without awareness, believers drift into routine, complacency, or spiritual dryness without noticing the shift.

This session helps you slow down and truly see where you are with God right now.

Why Awareness Matters

- You cannot grow where you are not honest.

- Awareness exposes blind spots before they become bondage.

- Awareness strengthens discernment and sensitivity to the Holy Spirit.

- Awareness positions you for breakthrough and restoration.

Warning Signs You May Be Spiritually Drifting

- You pray less often or with less passion.

- Scripture reading becomes inconsistent or rushed.

- Worship feels mechanical instead of meaningful.

- You avoid conviction or difficult spiritual conversations.

- You increasingly rely on your own strength.

- You feel spiritually tired but don't know why.

2. Worksheet: Personal Devotion Assessment

Devotional Area	Needs Improvement	Steady	Strong
Morning Prayer			
Evening Prayer			
Bible Reading			
Meditation			
Worship Time			
Journaling			
Listening for God			
Obedience to Promptings			

Reflections:

_____

_____

_____

_____

3. Worksheet: Prayer Life Analysis

Reflect honestly on your prayer habits.

- When do you pray most consistently?

- What hinders your prayer life?

- What strengthens your prayer time?

_____

_____

_____

_____

_____

4. Worksheet: Spiritual Warning Signs Checklist

Check the warning signs that apply to you:

☐ I've lost passion for prayer.

☐ I'm spiritually tired or overwhelmed.

☐ I avoid certain Scriptures or sermons.

☐ I feel disconnected from God.

☐ I struggle to focus spiritually.

☐ I feel easily irritated or emotionally unstable.

☐ I lack joy.

☐ I compromise in small ways.

☐ I rely more on self than the Holy Spirit.

Reflections:

_____

_____

_____

_____

_____

Section 3 — Understanding Strengths

1. Teaching Content: Recognizing God-Given Strengths

Spiritual strengths are the God-given abilities, graces, and consistent patterns of obedience that empower you to serve, grow, and fulfill your Kingdom assignment.

Strengths are not about personal glory—they are about stewarding well what God has entrusted to you.

Why Strengths Matter

- Strengths reveal your calling and purpose.

- Strengths show how God uniquely uses you.

- Strengths help build the Kingdom effectively.

- Strengths give confidence and clarity when serving.

- Strengths protect against burnout and confusion.

What Spiritual Strengths Often Look Like

- A strong prayer life or intercessory gifting

- Ability to encourage and uplift others

- Consistency in spiritual disciplines

- Strong faith during crisis

- Leadership, teaching, compassion, administration

- A heart for service, evangelism, or worship

Your strengths are signs of God's investment in you.

2. Worksheet: My Strengths Inventory

List the spiritual strengths you believe God has given you. Consider patterns that have shown up repeatedly in your life:

- _____

- _____

- _____

- _____

- _____

Ask yourself:

- What comes naturally to me spiritually?
- Where have I seen consistent growth?
- What do others affirm in me?

_____
_____
_____
_____
_____

3. Worksheet: Gifts, Talents & Graces Map
Rate or identify your abilities using the map below.

Gifts (Spiritual)	Talents (Natural)	Graces (Areas God Strengthens You)
_____	_____	_____
_____	_____	_____
_____	_____	_____
_____	_____	_____
_____	_____	_____

4. Worksheet: Where God Has Used Me Most
Think back over your life and ministry experience. List the places, moments, areas, or seasons where you know God used you in a powerful or consistent way:

- _____

- _____

- _____

- _____

5. Worksheet: My Ministry Value Profile

Circle the ministry values most important to you:

Prayer   Integrity   Service   Worship   Leadership   Teaching   Encouragement

Discipleship   Evangelism   Compassion   Excellence   Accountability

Why did you choose these values?

_____
_____
_____
_____

How do these values connect to your spiritual strengths?

_____
_____
_____
_____

Section 4 — Understanding Weaknesses

1. Teaching Content: Facing Spiritual Weaknesses with Honesty

Weaknesses are not signs of failure—they are areas where God desires to strengthen, heal, and mature you. Spiritual weakness becomes dangerous only when ignored, denied, or hidden.

This section helps you confront your weaknesses with humility and clarity so the Holy Spirit can transform them.

Why Recognizing Weakness Is Critical
- Weakness ignored becomes bondage.

- Weakness admitted becomes an opportunity for grace.

- Weakness revealed becomes a path to healing.

- Weakness evaluated becomes a strategy for growth.

- Weakness surrendered becomes strength.

The goal is not shame but transformation. God can only change what we are willing to confront.

Common Types of Spiritual Weaknesses

- Inconsistency in spiritual disciplines
- Emotional instability
- Unhealed trauma
- Lack of boundaries or people-pleasing
- Struggles with temptation or fleshly patterns
- Doubt, fear, or lack of trust
- Spiritual laziness or complacency
- Disobedience or delayed obedience

2. Worksheet: Personal Weakness Audit

Consider the areas of your spiritual life where you struggle most. Be honest and specific.

Areas where I feel spiritually weak:

- _____

- _____

Areas where I avoid accountability:

- _____

- _____

Areas where I am inconsistent:

- _____

- _____

Areas where I feel spiritually vulnerable:

- _____

- _____

3. Worksheet: Flesh vs. Spirit Struggles Chart

Use the chart below to identify patterns where the flesh and Spirit battle within you (see Galatians 5:17).

Struggle Area	Flesh Response	Spirit Response (Desired)
_____	_____	_____
_____	_____	_____
_____	_____	_____
_____	_____	_____
_____	_____	_____

4. Worksheet: Temptation Patterns Log

Temptation often follows patterns. Identifying them helps you build strategy and accountability.

Write about your patterns in the following areas:

Times of day or seasons when temptation is strongest:

- _____

- _____

- _____

Triggers or emotional states connected to temptation:

- _____

- _____

- _____

People, environments, or influences that weaken you:

- _____

- _____

- _____

Ways the enemy commonly attacks you:

- _____

- _____

- _____

5. Worksheet: Spiritual Discipline Gaps Checklist

Check the disciplines where you often struggle or lack consistency:

☐ Prayer consistency

☐ Bible reading consistency

☐ Fasting

☐ Worship outside of church

☐ Applying Scripture to daily decisions

☐ Maintaining godly boundaries

☐ Guarding my thoughts and emotions

☐ Accountability

☐ Serving regularly

☐ Guarding what I watch, listen to, and consume

6. Worksheet: Blind Spot Identification Tool

Blind spots are weaknesses others can see that you cannot. Use this worksheet to gain insight.

Questions to reflect on:

- What have others lovingly corrected me about?

___

___

___

- What feedback do I often ignore?

___

___

___

- What sins or habits repeat themselves?

___

___

___

- What do I justify instead of addressing?

___

___

___

- What patterns do I minimize or downplay?

___

___

___

Section 5 — Opportunities

1. Teaching Content: Recognizing God-Given Opportunities

Opportunities are divine openings, invitations, or moments God provides for your spiritual growth, ministry impact, or Kingdom assignment. Sometimes they appear obvious, but often they are subtle and require discernment.

Opportunities do not come randomly. They arrive as part of God's intentional development process for your life.

How to Recognize a God-Given Opportunity

- It aligns with Scripture and godly principles.
- It stretches you spiritually but does not compromise your integrity.
- It pushes you toward obedience and growth.
- It benefits others, not just yourself.
- It requires faith but produces peace in your spirit.
- It matches a season God is preparing you for (Ecclesiastes 3:1).

Types of Kingdom Opportunities

- Opportunities to grow in spiritual disciplines
- Opportunities to serve or volunteer in ministry
- Opportunities to be mentored or discipled
- Opportunities to lead, teach, or minister
- Opportunities to develop character and endurance
- Opportunities to evangelize or encourage others

2. Worksheet: Where God Is Opening Doors

List places where you sense God might be opening a door for growth, service, or leadership:

- _____

- _____

- _____

- _____

- _____

Reflection Questions:

• What has God been speaking to you about lately?

_____
_____
_____
_____
_____

• What new responsibilities or ideas keep arising?

_____
_____
_____
_____
_____

• What burdens or passions do you sense in prayer?

_____
_____
_____
_____
_____

3. Worksheet: Ministry Opportunity Assessment

Rate each area below based on how strongly you sense God pulling you toward it:

Ministry Area	1 (No Pull)	2	3	4	5 (Strong Pull)
Teaching/Preaching					
Evangelism					
Intercessory Prayer					
Youth Ministry					
Worship/Arts					
Helps Ministry					
Hospitality					
Leadership Development					
Outreach					
Discipleship					
Administration					
Counseling/Support					

Notes:

_____

_____

_____

_____

_____

_____

_____

_____

_____

4. Worksheet: Growth Opportunity Planner

Use this planner to identify and prepare for upcoming opportunities God may be presenting to you.

Skills or disciplines I need to develop:

- _____

- _____

- _____

- _____

- _____

- _____

People I may need to learn from or be mentored by:

- _____

- _____

- _____

- _____

- _____

- _____

Ministry areas where I feel drawn or burdened:

- _____

- _____

- _____

- _____

- _____

- _____

Steps I can take in the next 30 days:

- _____

- _____

- _____

- _____

- _____

- _____

5. Worksheet: Divine Timing Reflection Guide

Reflection on how God has been moving in your life during this season:

What season am I currently in spiritually?

_____

_____

_____

What opportunities seem to keep reappearing?

_____

_____

_____

Am I resisting something God is calling me to do?

_____

_____

_____

What fears or doubts are holding me back?

_____

_____

_____

Where do I sense peace, confirmation, or clarity?

_____

_____

_____

Section 6 — Threats

1. Teaching Content: Identifying Spiritual Threats

Threats are internal or external forces that attempt to weaken your walk with God, derail your spiritual growth, or distract you from your Kingdom assignment.

Some threats are obvious, but many are subtle - developing slowly over time. Recognizing them early allows you to stand firm against the enemy's strategies.

Common Types of Spiritual Threats

- Spiritual laziness or inconsistency
- Emotional instability, stress, burnout
- Toxic relationships or ungodly influences
- Fear, doubt, double-mindedness
- Unforgiveness or bitterness
- Spiritual warfare, temptation, demonic attack
- Pride, self-sufficiency, or isolation
- Distractions that drain time and focus

Threats do not mean defeat—they are alerts pointing to areas requiring vigilance, boundaries, or spiritual reinforcement.

2. Worksheet: Threat Identification Chart

Threat Type	Description	Impact on Spiritual Life

Reflections:

3. Worksheet: Early Warning Signs Checklist

Check any warning signs you have experienced recently:

☐ I feel spiritually numb or disconnected.

☐ I avoid prayer or Bible reading.

☐ I feel easily irritated or emotionally overwhelmed.

☐ I distance myself from church or accountability.

☐ I tolerate things I used to avoid.

☐ I hide certain behaviors or feelings.

☐ My consistency with God is slipping.

☐ I feel under spiritual attack.

☐ I am tempted in familiar patterns.

☐ I rely on myself more than the Holy Spirit.

Notes:

_____
_____
_____
_____
_____
_____
_____
_____
_____
_____
_____

4. Worksheet: Influence Audit

Everything influences you—people, places, media, habits, and environments. This audit helps you evaluate which influences strengthen you and which weaken you.

Influence	Strengthens Me	Weakens Me
_____	_____	_____
_____	_____	_____
_____	_____	_____
_____	_____	_____
_____	_____	_____
_____	_____	_____
_____	_____	_____
_____	_____	_____

5. Worksheet: Toxic Patterns Reflection

Patterns of behavior that harm my spiritual life:

- _____

- _____

- _____

Habits I know God is calling me to lay down:

- _____

- _____

- _____

Cycles that repeat when I am stressed or overwhelmed:

- _____

- _____

- _____

Ways I respond negatively during conflict or pressure:

- _____

- _____

- _____

6. Worksheet: Temptation Trigger Map
Identify the emotional, situational, or relational triggers that lead to temptation.

Emotional triggers (loneliness, anger, boredom):

_____

_____

_____

Situational triggers (late at night, isolated, stressed):

_____

_____

_____

_____

Relational triggers (specific people or groups):

___

___

___

___

Environmental triggers (places, settings, online spaces):

___

___

___

___

7. Worksheet: Boundary Setting Blueprint

Healthy boundaries protect your spiritual life from unnecessary threats, distractions, and temptations.

Boundaries I need with people:

___

___

___

___

Boundaries I need with time and priorities:

___

___

___

___

Boundaries I need with media and entertainment:

_____
_____
_____
_____

Boundaries I need spiritually:

_____
_____
_____
_____

8. Worksheet: Armor of God Strategy Worksheet
Based on Ephesians 6:10–18, reflect on how you can intentionally apply each piece of the armor of God.

• Belt of Truth — How I will walk in truth:

_____
_____
_____
_____

• Breastplate of Righteousness — Areas to pursue holiness:

_____
_____
_____
_____

- Gospel of Peace — How I will walk in peace:

- Shield of Faith — Attacks I must block with faith:

- Helmet of Salvation — Thoughts I must guard:

- Sword of the Spirit — Scriptures I must stand on:

• Prayer — How I will remain spiritually alert:

_____

_____

_____

_____

Section 7 — Session 3: Corrective Actions & Strategic Growth

1. Teaching Content: Turning Awareness into Action

Once you understand your strengths, weaknesses, opportunities, and threats, it's time to take intentional action. Spiritual growth does not happen automatically—it happens strategically. This section helps you build a clear, practical, Spirit-led action plan.

Corrective actions are not punishment—they are alignment. They help bring your life, habits, thoughts, and decisions into agreement with God's will.

What Effective Spiritual Growth Requires
- Honesty about where you truly are

- A clear plan for where you need to go

- Discipline and consistency

- Accountability

- Dependence on the Holy Spirit

Growth becomes intentional when you turn reflection into strategy.

2. Worksheet: Strength Development Plan

Identify your top strengths and list ways to cultivate and use them more effectively in ministry and personal growth:
My Top Strengths:

- _____

- _____

- _____

How I Currently Use These Strengths:

-
-
-

How I Can Use These Strengths More Effectively:

-
-
-

Areas Where These Strengths Can Make Me More Fruitful:

-
-
-

3. Worksheet: Weakness Reinforcement Strategy

For each weakness, identify a plan to strengthen it. Include spiritual disciplines, boundaries, accountability, and practical steps.

My Top Weaknesses:

-
-
-

Disciplines Needed to Strengthen These Weaknesses:

- _____

- _____

- _____

Boundaries Needed:

- _____

- _____

- _____

Support or Accountability Needed:

- _____

- _____

- _____

Steps I Will Take This Month:

- _____

- _____

- _____

4. Worksheet: Opportunity Activation Steps

Use this worksheet to turn opportunities into action. Every opportunity requires steps of faith and preparation.

Opportunities I Believe God Is Presenting:

_____

_____

_____

_____

Preparation Required:

_____

_____

_____

_____

People I Need to Connect With:

_____

_____

_____

_____

Skills I Need to Develop:

_____

_____

_____

_____

First Faith Step I Will Take:

_____

_____

_____

_____

5. Worksheet: Threat Neutralization Plan

Create a plan to minimize or eliminate spiritual threats. List the strategies, boundaries, and reinforcements needed to protect your spiritual life.

Threats I Need to Address:

- _____

- _____

- _____

- _____

Boundaries I Will Set:

- _____

- _____

- _____

- _____

Spiritual Disciplines I Will Strengthen:

- _____

- _____

- _____

- _____

People Who Will Hold Me Accountable:

- _____

- _____

- _____

- _____

Steps I Will Take Immediately:

- _____

- _____

- _____

- _____

6. Worksheet: Monthly Spiritual Goals Sheet
Use this sheet to set focused monthly goals.

Monthly Prayer Goal:

_____

_____

_____

_____

Monthly Bible Study Goal:

_____

_____

_____

_____

Monthly Ministry Goal:

Monthly Personal Development Goal:

Monthly Accountability Goal:

7. Worksheet: Accountability Partner Tool
Identify an accountability partner and outline how you will walk together in spiritual growth.

Name of Accountability Partner:

Why I chose this person:

Our meeting or check-in schedule:

_____
_____
_____

Areas they will hold me accountable:

_____
_____
_____

How I will communicate honestly:

_____
_____
_____

8. Worksheet: 30/60/90 Day Growth Plan

Use this structured plan to map out your next steps in spiritual growth.

30-Day Goals:

- _____

- _____

- _____

- _____

60-Day Goals:

- _____

- _____

- _____

- _____

90-Day Goals:

- _____

- _____

- _____

- _____

Notes:

_____
_____
_____
_____
_____
_____
_____
_____
_____

Section 8 — S.W.O.T. Charts

1. Full S.W.O.T. Chart (Blank)

Use this chart to complete your full Spiritual S.W.O.T. Analysis. Fill each quadrant honestly and prayerfully.

STRENGTHS

_____
_____
_____

WEAKNESSES

_____
_____
_____

OPPORTUNITIES

_____
_____
_____

THREATS

_____
_____
_____

2. Guided S.W.O.T. Chart (With Prompts)

This guided version includes prompts to help you think more deeply about each quadrant.

STRENGTHS
- What am I consistently good at?
- Where has God used me most?
- What spiritual disciplines am I strong in?

WEAKNESSES
- Where do I struggle most?
- What drains me spiritually?
- What habits or sins need attention?

OPPORTUNITIES
- What doors is God opening?
- What skills can I develop?
- Who can mentor or teach me?

THREATS
- What influences weaken me?
- What patterns keep repeating?
- What is the enemy using to attack me?

Notes:

_____
_____
_____
_____

3. Mini S.W.O.T. Charts

Use these mini charts for specific topics such as marriage, finances, ministry, leadership, or emotional health.

Mini S.W.O.T. Chart 1

STRENGTHS   WEAKNESSES
_____   _____

OPPORTUNITIES   THREATS
_____   _____

Notes:

_____
_____
_____

Mini S.W.O.T. Chart 2

STRENGTHS   WEAKNESSES
_____   _____

OPPORTUNITIES   THREATS
_____   _____

Notes:

_____
_____
_____

Mini S.W.O.T. Chart 3

STRENGTHS   WEAKNESSES
_____   _____

OPPORTUNITIES   THREATS
_____   _____

Notes:

_____
_____
_____

Section 9 — Prayers, Scriptures & Declarations

1. Scriptures for Strength

- Philippians 4:13 — I can do all things through Christ which strengtheneth me.

- Isaiah 40:31 — They that wait upon the LORD shall renew their strength.

- Psalm 27:1 — The LORD is the strength of my life; of whom shall I be afraid?

- Ephesians 6:10 — Be strong in the Lord, and in the power of his might.

2. Scriptures for Deliverance

- Psalm 34:17 — The righteous cry, and the LORD heareth, and delivereth them.

- Psalm 107:6 — Then they cried unto the LORD in their trouble, and he delivered them.

- John 8:36 — If the Son therefore shall make you free, ye shall be free indeed.

- Nahum 1:7 — The LORD is good, a strong hold in the day of trouble.

3. Scriptures for Wisdom

- James 1:5 — If any of you lack wisdom, let him ask of God.

- Proverbs 3:5–6 — Trust in the LORD with all thine heart.

- Proverbs 4:7 — Wisdom is the principal thing; therefore get wisdom.

- Colossians 1:9 — Be filled with the knowledge of his will in all wisdom.

4. Scriptures for Victory

- 1 Corinthians 15:57 — Thanks be to God, which giveth us the victory.

- Romans 8:37 — We are more than conquerors through him that loved us.

- Psalm 60:12 — Through God we shall do valiantly.

- Deuteronomy 20:4 — The LORD your God is he that goeth with you to fight for you.

Reflections:

_____

_____

_____

_____

5. Prayers for Alignment

- Father, align my heart with Your will and desires.

- Lord, remove anything in me that does not reflect You.

- Holy Spirit, guide my decisions, thoughts, and priorities.

- God, help me walk in obedience every day.

Write Your Prayer:

_____

_____

_____

_____

_____

_____

6. Prayers for Spiritual Growth

- Lord, deepen my hunger for Your Word.

- Help me grow stronger in spiritual discipline.

- Develop my character and make me more like Christ.

- Expand my capacity to serve with excellence.

Write Your Prayer:

_____

_____

_____

_____

_____

_____

7. Prayers for Protection
- Lord, cover me with Your divine protection.

- Guard my mind from the enemy's lies.

- Strengthen me to resist temptation.

- Surround my family with Your angels.

Write Your Prayer:

_____

_____

_____

_____

_____

8. Daily Declarations
☐ I am who God says I am.

☐ I walk in spiritual strength and wisdom.

☐ I am growing daily in Christ.

☐ I reject every attack of the enemy.

☐ I embrace every opportunity God gives me.

☐ I am covered, called, and chosen.

☐ I will fulfill God's purpose for my life.

Personal Daily Declaration:

_____

_____

_____

_____

Section 10 — Final Reflection & Commitment

1. Final Reflection Questions

Use this space to reflect deeply on what God has shown you throughout this Spiritual S.W.O.T. journey.

1. What has God revealed to me about my strengths?

_____
_____
_____

2. What weaknesses is God calling me to surrender or strengthen?

_____
_____
_____

3. What opportunities is God opening for my spiritual and ministry growth?

_____
_____
_____

4. What threats must I guard against more intentionally?

_____
_____
_____

5. How have I grown in awareness, discipline, and obedience?

_____
_____
_____

6. What surprised me during this process?

_____
_____
_____

7. What is God calling me to start, stop, or continue?

_____
_____
_____

2. Personal Commitment Covenant

This covenant is a personal commitment between you and God as you move forward in spiritual growth.

I, _____, commit myself to continued spiritual growth, obedience, and alignment with God's will for my life. I will intentionally develop my strengths, address my weaknesses, embrace God-given opportunities, and guard against all spiritual threats. I submit my plans, desires, and future to the leading of the Holy Spirit. With God's help, I will walk worthy of the calling placed on my life.

Signature: _____

Date: _____

3. My Spiritual Transformation Statement

Write a bold, faith-filled declaration summarizing the transformation you believe God is producing in your life as a result of this process:

_____
_____
_____
_____

4. Prayer of Dedication

Father, in the name of Jesus, I dedicate my life, my growth, my purpose, and my future to You. Strengthen me where I am weak, build me where I am broken, and guide me into the fullness of who You have called me to be. Help me to walk in discipline, integrity, consistency, and faith. Surround me with Your protection, fill me with Your wisdom, and empower me to fulfill Your purpose for my life. I declare that my life belongs to You, and with Your help, I will grow, mature, and walk in victory. In Jesus' name, Amen.

Thank You for Completing the Spiritual S.W.O.T. Journey

Remember: Growth is a lifelong process. Continue seeking God, evaluating your walk, and aligning with His will daily.

You are called, chosen, equipped, and empowered to live a life of purpose and impact.

Your Journey from Reflection to Transformation Begins Here

Made in the USA
Middletown, DE
22 February 2026

28641575R00024